Contents

My Racist Introduction

Chapter 1: Definitions

Chapter 2: Dueling Consciousness

Chapter 3: Power

Chapter 4: Biology

Chapter 5: Ethnicity

Chapter 6: Body

Chapter 7: Culture

Chapter 8: Behavior

Chapter 9: Color

Chapter 10: White

Chapter 11: Black

Chapter 12: Class

Chapter 13: Space

Chapter 14: Gender

Chapter 15: Sexuality

Chapter 16: Failure

Chapter 17: Success

Chapter 18: Survival

Book 3

GENDER

GENDER RACISM: A powerful collection of racist policies that lead to inequity between race-genders and are substantiated by racist ideas about race-genders.

GENDER ANTIRACISM: A powerful collection of antiracist policies that lead to equity between race-genders and are substantiated by antiracist ideas about race-genders.

NO ONE OVERLOOKED the sheer size of her intellect, which was even more immediately apparent than her tall, full build and striking makeup. No one overlooked Kaila at all. She did not tuck away a single aspect of herself by the time I met her at Temple. No self-censoring. No closeting of her lesbian feminism in a Black space that could be antagonizing to lesbianism and feminism. No ambiguity for misinterpretation. All badass Joan Morgan "chickenhead" giving no fucks. All warrior poet giving all fucks, like her idol, Audre Lorde. Kaila was entirely herself, and her Laila Ali intellect wished for the world to voice a problem with what they saw.

Kaila had no problem telling you about yourself. Her legendary impersonations of African American studies students and faculty were as funny as they were accurate. I always wanted her to do an impersonation of me, but I was too scared and insecure to see what she saw.

Kaila held court with Yaba, whose roaring, full-bodied laughter often filled the room. Their back-and-forth jokes were as bad for victims as Venus and Serena Williams's matches were bad for tennis balls. When I sat down for a long talk—or, rather, to listen and learn—my mouth seemed to always be open, in laughter at their jokes or jaw-dropping wonder over their insights. They sat as the royal court of African American studies graduate students. Everyone feared or respected or battled them. I feared and respected them, too scared and awed to battle.

Yaba's irrepressible Blackness governed our Blacker-than-thou space. Blacker than thou not because of her Ghanaian features, her down-home New Orleans air, or her mixes of African garb and African American fashion. Not because she danced as comfortably to the beat of West Indian cultures as she did to her own. She seemed to have an encyclopedic knowledge of Black people: the most ethnically antiracist person in my new world. As up to date on Black American popular culture as African politics, as equipped to debate the intricacies of the rise of Beyoncé as she could the third rise of Black feminism, as comfortable explaining the origins of Haitian Creole as the conflicts between the Yoruba and Igbo of Nigeria. I always felt so ignorant around her.

—

I ARRIVED AT Temple as a racist, sexist homophobe. Not exactly friend material for these two women. But they saw the potential in me I did not see in myself.

My ideas of gender and sexuality reflected those of my parents. They did not raise me not to be a homophobe. They rarely talked about gay and lesbian people. Ideas often dance a cappella. Their silence erased queer existence as thoroughly as integrationists erased the reality of integrated White spaces.

On gender, Dad's perception of masculine strength did not derive from the perceived weakness of women. Maybe because Ma made no bones about her strength. She'd weight-lifted ever since I could remember. She carried heavy bags into the house, letting the three six-footers she lived with know that even at five foot three and 120 pounds, she was no physical slouch. Dad had always been more emotional and affectionate than Ma. Dad comforted my brother and me when we got hurt. Ma told us to suck it up, like the time I came in crying about breaking my wrist. She ordered me back outside to finish the basketball game.

Dad often joked at church about Ma being the CFO of the family. While other patriarchal men laughed, Dad was serious. She was. At other times, Dad's sexist ideas demanded he lead and Ma's sexist ideas submitted. She would call him the head of the household. He would accept the calling.

My parents did not strictly raise me to be a Black patriarch. I became a Black patriarch because my parents and the world around me did not strictly raise me to be a Black feminist. Neither my parents nor I came up in an age conducive to teaching Black feminism to a Black boy, if there ever was such an age. There seemed to be a low-level war being waged between the genders, maybe most clearly articulated in our popular culture. I was born the year of Alice Walker's *The Color Purple,* a seminal work of Black feminist art, but one that many Black male critics saw as a hit job on Black masculinity. I entered adolescence the year Black women were hitting theaters for a cathartic tour of Black male maltreatment, *Waiting to Exhale.* But the latest conflict had deeper roots, perhaps germinating in the summer of 1965, when the media got ahold of "The Negro Family: The Case for National Action," a government report written by President Johnson's assistant secretary of labor, Daniel Patrick Moynihan.

Nearly one-fourth of Black families were headed by women, twice the rate for White families, Moynihan warned, as the media swooned about the "broken" Black family. "The Negro community has been forced into a matriarchal structure which...imposes a crushing burden on the Negro male," producing a "tangle of pathology,"

Moynihan asserted. Moynihan called for national action to employ and empower Black men, who had been emasculated by discrimination and matriarchal Black women. "Keeping the Negro 'in his place' can be translated as keeping the Negro male in his place: The female was not a threat to anyone," Moynihan wrote.

"The reverberations" from the Moynihan report "were disastrous," historian Deborah Gray White once wrote. Racist patriarchs, from White social scientists to Black husbands, demanded the submission of Black women to uplift the race. A command in *Ebony* magazine became popular: The "immediate goal of the Negro woman today should be the establishment of a strong family unit in which the father is the dominant person." A decade later, Black patriarchs and White social scientists were still touting the idea that Black men had it worse than Black women. Racism had "clearly" and "largely focused" on the Black male, sociologist Charles Herbert Stember argued in his 1976 book, *Sexual Racism: The Emotional Barrier to an Integrated Society*. An America of integrated (White) spaces had not been achieved because at racism's core was the "sexual rejection of the racial minority, the conscious attempt on the part of the majority to prevent interracial cohabitation," he wrote. The White man's sexual jealousy of the Black man was the key.

For too many Black men, the Black Power movement that emerged after the Moynihan report became a struggle against White men for Black power over Black women. Dad witnessed this power struggle, after being raised by a single Black mother who never called him or his brother the head of the household, like other patriarchal single moms did. One day in 1969, Dad had been singing inside a storefront church. He stepped outside for air and confronted a Black Panther assaulting his girlfriend. On another day, in the summer of 1971, Dad and a girlfriend before Ma ventured up to the

Harlem Temple of the Nation of Islam. The Nation had piqued Dad's interest. They were eating with one of the ministers. Dad's girlfriend said something. The minister smacked her and smacked from his mouth, "Women are not to speak in the presence of men." Dad sprang out of his chair and had to be restrained and strong-armed out of the temple.

In spite of everything, Dad and Ma could not help but join the interracial force policing the sexuality of young Black mothers. They were two of the millions of liberals and conservatives aghast at the growing percentage of Black children being born into single-parent households in the 1970s and 1980s—aghast even though my dad turned out just fine. The panic around the reported numbers of single-parent households was based on a host of faulty or untested premises: that two bad parents would be better than one good one, that the presence of an abusive Black father is better for the child than his absence, that having a second income for a child trumps all other factors, that all of the single parents were Black women, that none of these absent fathers were in prison or the grave, that Black mothers never hid the presence of Black fathers in their household to keep their welfare for the child.

In time for the midterm elections in 1994, political scientist Charles Murray made sure Americans knew the percentage of Black children born into single-parent households "has now reached 68 percent." Murray blamed the "welfare system." My parents and other liberals blamed sexual irresponsibility, a shameful disregard for the opportunities born of 1960s activism, pathologizing poverty, and a disconnect from the premarital abstinence of Christ. They were all wrong on so many levels. The increasing percentage of Black babies born into single-parent households was not due to single Black mothers having more children but to married Black women having fewer children over the course of the twentieth century. Ma could see that decline in her family. Ma's married paternal grandmother had sixteen children in the 1910s and 1920s. Ma's married mother had six children in the 1940s and 1950s. My mother had two children in the early 1980s—as did two of her three married sisters.

Ma and Dad and countless Americans were disconnected from racial reality and leapt to demonize this class of single mothers. Only Black feminists like Dorothy Roberts and Angela Davis defended them.

—

ON OTHER ISSUES, Ma sometimes put up a feminist defense. It was early August 1976, the Tuesday before the Saturday my parents were scheduled to wed. Running down the ceremony, Pastor Wilfred Quinby recited the Christian wedding vows for my parents. "Husbands, love your wives, and wives, obey your husbands."

"I'm not obeying him!" Ma interjected. "What!" Pastor Quinby said in shock, turning to look at my father. "What!" Dad said, turning to look at my mother.

"The only man I obeyed was my father, when I was a child," she nearly shouted, staring into Dad's wide eyes. "You are not my father and I'm not a child!"

The clock was ticking. Would Dad whip out Bible verses on women's submission and fight for the sexist idea? Would he crawl away and look for another woman, who would submit? Dad chose a different option: the only option that could have yielded their marriage of more than four decades. He slowly picked up his jaw, popped his eyes back in their sockets, and offered Ma an equitable solution.

"How about: Are you willing to submit one to another?" he asked.

Ma nodded. She liked the sound of "one to another," integrating the Christian concept of submission with feminist equity. My parents wrote their own wedding vows. Pastor Quinby married them as scheduled.

—

DAD SHOULD NOT have been shocked at Ma's resistance. For some time, Ma had been rethinking Christian sexism. After they wed, Ma attended "consciousness-raising conferences" for Christian women in Queens. What Kimberly Springer calls the "Black feminist movement" had finally burst through the sexist dams of Christian churches. Black feminists rejected the prevailing Black patriarchal idea that the primary activist role of Black women was submitting to their husbands and producing more Black babies for the "Black nation." Through groups like the Black Women's Alliance (1970) and the National Black Feminist Organization (1973), through Black women's caucuses in Black power and women's liberation groups, Black feminists fought sexism in Black spaces and racism in women's spaces. They developed their own spaces, and a Black feminist consciousness for Black women's liberation, for the liberation of humanity.

Black queer activists, too, had been marginalized after they launched the gay-liberation movement through the Stonewall rebellion in Manhattan in 1969. Braving homophobia in Black spaces and racism in queer spaces, antiracist queer people formed their own spaces. Perhaps the most antiracist queer space of the era may have also been the most antiracist feminist space of the era. In the summer of 1974, a group of Boston Black women separated from the National Black Feminist Organization to form the Combahee River Collective, named for the Combahee River slave raid of 1863 led by Harriet Tubman. They revived the unadulterated freedom politics of General Tubman. In 1977, they shared their views, in a statement drafted by Barbara

Smith, Demita Frazier, and Beverly Smith. The Combahee River Collective Statement embodied queer liberation, feminism, and antiracism, like perhaps no other public statement in American history. They did not want Black women to be viewed as inferior or superior to any other group. "To be recognized as human, levelly human, is enough.

"Our politics initially sprang from the shared belief that Black women are inherently valuable," they wrote. "No other ostensibly progressive movement has ever considered our specific oppression as a priority....We realize that the only people who care enough about us to work consistently for our liberation are us." Maria Stewart, America's first feminist known to give a public address to a coed audience, considered and prioritized the specific oppression of Black women in her daring speeches in the early 1830s in Boston. So did Sojourner Truth and Frances Harper, before and after the Civil War. So did Ida B. Wells and Anna Julia Cooper, in the early 1900s. So did Frances Beal, who audaciously proclaimed in 1968, "the black woman in America can justly be described as a 'slave of a slave,'" the victim of the "double jeopardy" of racism and sexism. This position paper joined an anthology of pieces in 1970 by women like Nikki Giovanni, Audre Lorde, and a young Mississippi prodigy named Alice Walker. Editor Toni Cade Bambara, a Rutgers literary scholar, ensured *The Black Woman* best reflected "the preoccupations of the contemporary Black woman in this country," including setting "the record straight on the matriarch and the evil Black bitch."

But 1991—the year Anita Hill accused U.S. Supreme Court nominee Clarence Thomas of sexual harassment—proved to be the pivotal year of Black feminist scholars. They constructed terminology that named the specific oppression facing Black women, which Black feminists from Maria Stewart to Anna Julia Cooper to Angela

Davis had been identifying for more than a century. Behind the scenes of what Thomas mind-bogglingly called a "high-tech lynching" and Black feminists' frontline defense of Hill, Afro-Dutch scholar Philomena Essed worked on a project that would help define what was happening. She published her reflections on in-depth interviews she'd conducted with Black women in the United States and the Netherlands in *Understanding Everyday Racism.* "In discussing the experiences of Black women, is it sexism or is it racism?" Essed asked. "These two concepts narrowly intertwine and combine under certain conditions into one, hybrid phenomenon. Therefore, it is useful to speak of *gendered racism.*"

In 1991, UCLA critical race theorist Kimberlé Williams Crenshaw further explored this notion of "intersectionality." That year, she published "Mapping the Margins: Intersectionality, Identity Politics, and Violence Against Women of Color" in the *Stanford Law Review,* based on her address at the Third National Conference on Women of Color and the Law in 1990. "Feminist efforts to politicize experiences of women and antiracist efforts to politicize experiences of people of color have frequently proceeded as though the issues and experiences they each detail occur on mutually exclusive terrains," Crenshaw theorized. "Although racism and sexism readily intersect in the lives of real people, they seldom do in feminist and antiracist practices."

Racist (and sexist) power distinguishes race-genders, racial (or gender) groups at the intersection of race and gender. Women are a gender. Black people are a race. When we identify Black women, we are identifying a race-gender. A sexist policy produces inequities between women and men. A racist policy produces inequities between racial groups. When a policy produces inequities between race-genders, it is gendered racism, or gender racism for short.

To be antiracist is to reject not only the hierarchy of races but of race-genders. To be feminist is to reject not only the hierarchy of genders but of race-genders. To truly be antiracist is to be feminist. To truly be feminist is to be antiracist. To be antiracist (and feminist) is to level the different race-genders, is to root the inequities between the equal race-genders in the policies of gender racism.

Gender racism was behind the growing number of involuntary sterilizations of Black women by eugenicist physicians—two hundred thousand cases in 1970, rising to seven hundred thousand in 1980. Gender racism produced the current situation of Black women with some collegiate education making less than White women with only high school degrees; Black women having to earn advanced degrees before they earn more than White women with bachelor's degrees; and the median wealth of single White women being $42,000 compared to $100 for single Black women. Native women and Black women experience poverty at a higher rate than any other race-gender group. Black and Latinx women still earn the least, while White and Asian men earn the most. Black women are three to four times more likely to die from pregnancy-related causes than are White women. A Black woman with an advanced degree is more likely to lose her baby than a White woman with less than an eighth-grade education. Black women remain twice as likely to be incarcerated as White women.

Gender racism impacts White women and male groups of color, whether they see it or not. White women's resistance to Black feminism and intersectional theory has been self-destructive, preventing resisters from understanding their own oppression. The intersection of racism and sexism, in some cases, oppresses White women. For example, sexist notions of "real women" as weak and racist notions of White women as the idealized woman intersect to produce the gender-racist idea that the pinnacle of womanhood is the weak White woman. This is the gender racism that caused millions of men and women to hate the strong White woman running for president in 2016, Hillary Clinton. Or to give another example, the opposite of the gender racism of the unvirtuous hypersexual Black woman is the virtuous asexual White woman, a racial construct that has constrained and controlled the White woman's sexuality (as it nakedly tainted the Black woman's sexuality as un-rape-able). White-male interest in lynching Black-male rapists of White women was as much about controlling the sexuality of White women as it was about controlling the sexuality of Black men. Racist White patriarchs were re-creating the slave era all over again, making it illicit for White women to cohabitate with Black men at the same time as racist White (and Black) men were raping Black women. And the slave era remains, amid the hollow cries of race pride drowning out the cries of the sexually assaulted. Gender racism is behind the thinking that when one defends White male abusers like Trump and Brett Kavanaugh one is defending White people; when one defends Black male abusers like Bill Cosby and R. Kelly one is defending Black people.

Male resistance to Black feminism and intersectional theory has been similarly self-destructive, preventing resisters from understanding our specific oppression. The intersection of racism and sexism, in some cases, oppresses men of color. Black men reinforce oppressive tropes by reinforcing certain sexist ideas. For example, sexist notions of "real men" as strong and racist notions of Black men as not really men intersect to produce the gender racism of the weak Black man, inferior to the pinnacle of manhood, the strong White man.

Sexist notions of men as more naturally dangerous than women (since women are considered naturally fragile, in need of protection) and racist notions of Black people as more dangerous than White people intersect to produce the gender racism of the hyperdangerous Black man, more dangerous than the White man, the Black woman, and (the pinnacle of innocent frailty) the White woman. No defense is stronger than the frail tears of innocent White womanhood. No prosecution is stronger than the case for inherently guilty Black manhood. These ideas of gender racism transform every innocent Black male into a criminal and every White female criminal into Casey Anthony, the White woman a Florida jury exonerated in 2011, against all evidence, for killing her three-year-old child. White women get away with murder and Black men spend years in prisons for wrongful convictions. After the imprisonment of Black men dropped 24 percent between 2000 and 2015, Black men were still nearly six times more likely than White men, twenty-five times more likely than Black women, and fifty times more likely than White women to be incarcerated. Black men raised in the top 1 percent by millionaires are as likely to be incarcerated as White men raised in households earning $36,000.

—

"Contemporary feminist and antiracist discourses have failed to consider intersectional identities such as women of color," Kimberlé Crenshaw wrote in 1991. All racial groups are a collection of intersectional identities differentiated by gender, sexuality, class, ethnicity, skin color, nationality, and culture, among a series of other identifiers. Black women first recognized their own intersectional identity. Black feminists first theorized the intersection of two forms of bigotry: sexism and racism. Intersectional theory now gives all of humanity the ability to understand the intersectional oppression of their identities, from poor Latinx to Black men to White women to Native lesbians to transgender Asians. A theory for Black women is a theory for humanity. No wonder Black feminists have been saying from the beginning that when humanity becomes serious about the freedom of Black women, humanity becomes serious about the freedom of humanity.

Intersectional Black identities are subjected to what Crenshaw described as the intersection of racism and other forms of bigotry, such as ethnocentrism, colorism, sexism, homophobia, and transphobia. My journey to being an antiracist first recognized the intersectionality of my ethnic racism, and then my bodily racism, and then my cultural racism, and then my color racism, and then my class racism, and, when I entered graduate school, my gender racism and queer racism.

SEXUALITY

QUEER RACISM: A powerful collection of racist policies that lead to inequity between race-sexualities and are substantiated by racist ideas about race-sexualities.

QUEER ANTIRACISM: A powerful collection of antiracist policies that lead to equity between race-sexualities and are substantiated by antiracist ideas about race-sexualities.

RACIST (AND HOMOPHOBIC) power distinguishes race-sexualities, racial (or sexuality) groups at the intersection of race and sexuality. Homosexuals are a sexuality. Latinx people are a race. Latinx homosexuals are a race-sexuality. A homophobic policy produces inequities between heterosexuals and homosexuals. A racist policy produces inequities between racial groups. Queer racism produces inequities between race-sexualities. Queer racism produces a situation where 32 percent of children being raised by Black male same-sex couples live in poverty, compared to 14 percent of children being raised by White male same-sex couples, 13 percent of children raised by Black heterosexuals, and 7 percent of children raised by White heterosexuals. For children being raised by female same-sex couples who live in poverty, the racial disparity is nearly as wide. These children of Black queer couples are more likely to live in poverty because their parents are more likely than Black heterosexual and White queer couples to be poor.

Homophobia cannot be separated from racism. They've intersected for ages. British physician Havelock Ellis is known for popularizing the term "homosexual." In his first medical treatise on homosexuality, *Studies in the Psychology of Sex* (1897), he wrote about "the question of sex—with the racial questions that rest on it." He regarded homosexuality as a congenital physiological abnormality, just as he regarded criminality at the time. Ellis adored the father of criminology, Italian physician Cesare Lombroso, who claimed criminals are born, not bred, and that people of color are by nature criminals. In 1890, Ellis published a popular summary of Lombroso's writings.

Ellis spent many years defending against the criminalization of White homosexuality. Following racist scholars, Ellis used comparative anatomy of women's bodies to evidence the biological differences between the sexualities. "As regards the sexual organs it seems possible," Ellis wrote, "to speak more definitively of inverted women than of inverted men." At the time, racist physicians were contrasting the "bound together" clitoris of "Aryan American women" that "goes with higher civilization" and the "free" clitoris "in negresses" that goes with "highly domesticated animals." Homophobic physicians were supposing that "inverted" lesbians "will in practically every instance disclose an abnormally prominent clitoris," wrote New York City prison doctor Perry M. Lichtenstein. Racist ideas suggesting Black people are more hypersexual than White people and homophobic ideas suggesting queer people are more hypersexual than heterosexuals intersect to produce the queer racism of the most hypersexual race-sexuality, the Black queer. Their imagined biological stamp: the abnormally prominent clitoris, which "is particularly so in colored women," Lichtenstein added.

—

WECKEA WAS MY best friend at Temple. We were both brown-skinned with locs and hailed from prideful HBCUs. I usually befriended laid-back and calm people like him. He usually befriended daring and silly people like me. We were both curious by nature, but Weckea was as inquisitive a person as I had ever met. He wanted to know everything and damn near did. The only thing he seemed to love as much as a good idea was a good laugh. He was a few years older than me, and it did not take long for me to look up to him intellectually, in the way I looked up to Kaila and Yaba.

We arrived at Temple in the same cohort—Weckea, myself, and another student, Raena. We banded together.

On a rare day when Raena and I ate lunch together without Weckea, the two of us sat outside, near campus, probably delighting in the warm arrival of spring, probably in 2006. We both had food before us. First gossip and small talk and then, out of nowhere: "You know Weckea is gay, right." She barely looked up at me as she said it. Her eyes focused as she gobbled food.

"No, I didn't know that," I said, my voice breaking.

"Well, it's not a big deal he didn't tell you, right?"

"Right." I looked away. Cars honked. Peopled strolled by. An ambulance was coming. For me?

I glanced back at Raena, her chin tucked, eating. Wondering why she'd told me this. I did not see a friendly face of concern as I twitched in my chair. I saw a blankness, if not a face of satisfaction. Was she trying to break up my friendship with Weckea?

Neither of us had much to say after that. Mission accomplished on her part. Weckea's homosexuality made sense, as I thought about it. He had never spoken about dating a woman. When I asked, he deflected. I'd chalked it up to his extreme privacy. He would describe women as pretty or not so pretty but never in a sexual manner, which I chalked up to his conservatism. He was not so conservative after all.

I thought about Black gay men running around having unprotected sex all the time. But Weckea did not seem sex-crazed or reckless. I thought about this hypersexuality and recklessness causing so many Black gay men to contract HIV. I thought wrong. Black gay men are less likely to have condomless sex than White gay men. They are less likely to use drugs like poppers or crystal methamphetamine during sex, which heighten the risk of HIV infections.

I had been around gay Black men before, in FACES, a modeling troupe I'd joined at FAMU. But the gay Black men in the troupe (or, better yet, the ones I thought were gay) had what I thought of as a feminine streak to them: the way they moved, their makeup, the way they struggled to dap me up. They pinged my gaydar. Everything about my modeling troupe pinged the gaydar of my friends. My modeling ended up being the only thing my friends joked on more than my orange eyes. But they thought my orange eyes were "gay," too.

I assumed Black gay men performed femininity. I did not know that some gay men, like Weckea, perform masculinity and actually prefer gay men who perform femininity for partners. I did not know (and feminists like Kaila and Yaba were teaching me) about gender being an authentic performance; that the ways women and men traditionally act are not tied to their biology; that men can authentically perform femininity as effectively as women can authentically perform masculinity. Authentically, meaning they are not acting, as the transphobic idea assumes. They are being who they are, defying society's gender conventions. I learned this, once and for all, through my other close friendship at Temple, with a butch Black lesbian from Texas. I talked about women with Monica in the way I could not with Weckea. We were drawn to the same women. When we got to joking and relating our romantic experiences, my conversations with Monica did not sound too different from my conversations with my heterosexual male friends at FAMU.

—

MY MIND TURNED to introspection. Why had Weckea not told me? Why didn't he feel comfortable sharing his sexuality with me? Maybe he sensed my homophobia—in fact, he probably heard it in my rhetoric. He listened intently. He seemed to never forget anything.

In subsequent years, Weckea prided himself on showing off his "gaydar," pointing out to me closeted or down-low people at Temple. But Weckea was equally adept at identifying homophobia and taking the necessary precautions. He must have been protecting himself—and our early friendship—from my homophobia. Now I had a choice: my homophobia or my best friend. I could not have both for long. I chose Weckea and the beginning of our long friendship. I chose the beginning of the rest of my lifelong striving against the homophobia of my upbringing, a lifelong striving to be a queer antiracist.

Queer antiracism is equating all the race-sexualities, striving to eliminate the inequities between the race-sexualities. We cannot be antiracist if we are homophobic or transphobic. We must continue to "affirm that all Black lives matter," as the co-founder of Black Lives Matter, Opal Tometi, once said. All Black lives include those of poor transgender Black women, perhaps the most violated and oppressed of all the Black intersectional groups. The average U.S. life expectancy of a transgender woman of color is thirty-five years. The racial violence they face, the transphobia they face as they seek to live freely, is unfathomable. I started learning about their freedom fight from the personal stories of transgender activist Janet Mock. But I opened up to their fight on that day I opened to saving my friendship with Weckea.

I am a cisgendered Black heterosexual male —"cisgender" meaning my gender identity corresponds to my birth sex, in contrast to transgender people, whose gender identity does not correspond to their birth sex. To be queer antiracist is to understand the privileges of my cisgender, of my masculinity, of my heterosexuality, of their intersections. To be queer antiracist is to serve as an ally to transgender people, to intersex people, to women, to the non-gender-conforming, to homosexuals, to their intersections, meaning listening, learning, and being led by their equalizing ideas, by their equalizing policy campaigns, by their power struggle for equal opportunity. To be queer antiracist is to see that policies protecting Black transgender women are as critically important as policies protecting the political ascendancy of queer White males. To be queer antiracist is to see the new wave of both religious-freedom laws and voter-ID laws in Republican states as taking away the rights of queer people. To be queer antiracist is to see homophobia, racism, and queer racism—not the queer person, not the queer space—as the problem, as abnormal, as unnatural.

—

THEY SEEMED TO always be there—Yaba and Kaila—sitting around one of those tables near the entrance of Gladfelter Hall, sometimes with fellow doctoral students Danielle and Sekhmet. I usually caught these women on a smoke break or lunch break or dinner break from working together in Gladfelter's computer lab. They were finishing their doctorates in African American studies, nearing the end of a journey I was beginning at Temple.

Whenever Kaila and Yaba were seated there— whenever they were anywhere—their presence was unmistakable, memorable and unsettling and inspiring. I could go to war with them at my side. I learned from them that I am not a defender of Black people if I am not sharply defending Black women, if I am not sharply defending queer Blacks. The two of them exerted their influence on our department's events. When our department brought in speakers for a public event, they came. When graduate students shared their research at an event, they came. When there was an out-of-town Black studies conference, they came. When they came, let's just say they ensured that when patriarchal ideas arose, when homophobic ideas were put out there, when racist ideas came and intersected, they would come for those ideas like piranhas coming for their daily meal. I watched, stunned, in awe of their intellectual attacks. I call them attacks, but in truth they were defenses, defending Black womanhood and the humanity of queer Blacks. They were respectful and measured if the victimizer was respectful and measured with them. But I call them attacks because I felt personally attacked. They were attacking my gender racism about Black women, my queer racism about queer Blacks, my gender and queer racism about queer Black women.

I did not want to ever be their prey.

I binge-read every author they mentioned in their public exchanges and in their private exchanges with me. I gobbled up Audre Lorde, E. Patrick Johnson, bell hooks, Joan Morgan, Dwight McBride, Patricia Hill Collins, and Kimberlé Crenshaw like my life depended on it. My life *did* depend on it. I wanted to overcome my gender racism, my queer racism. But I had to be willing to do for Black women and queer Blacks what I had been doing for Black men and Black heterosexuals, which meant first of all learning more—and then defending them like my heroes had.

They were the darkness that scared me. I wanted to run away whenever I came off the elevator, turned the corner, and spotted Yaba and Kaila, whenever I approached the building and they were there. They warmly tossed smiles and greetings as I walked by not fast enough, forcing me to awkwardly toss them back.

Sometimes they stopped me in small talk. Over time, they let me join them in long talk, unnerving me the most. It is best to challenge ourselves by dragging ourselves before people who intimidate us with their brilliance and constructive criticism. I didn't think about that. I wanted to run away. They did not let me run away, and I am grateful now because of it.

These women were everything they were not supposed to be, in my patriarchal and homophobic mind. Queer people are run by sex, not ideas. Queer people are abnormal. Feminists hate men. Feminists want female supremacy. But these Black feminists obviously liked me, a male. They were as ideological as they were sexual as they were normal. They did not speak of women ruling men. They spoke of gender and queer equity and freedom and mutuality and complementarity and power. Their jokes and attacks knew no gender or sexuality. If anything, they were harder on women. They were harder on queer people like Raena. They saw through her long before Weckea and I did.

No one seemed to incite them more than "patriarchal women"—really, patriarchal White women standing behind racist White patriarchs. I can only imagine what they thought years later, watching Kayla Moore defend her husband, Alabama's U.S. Senate candidate Roy Moore, who had been accused of pedophilia and sexual assaults, who was asked on the campaign trail in 2017 when America was last great. "I think it was great at the time when families were united—even though we had slavery," he said. "Our families were strong, our country had direction." This was long before we had so many women publicly attacking the women saying #MeToo. Patriarchal women, as a term, made no sense to me back then, like the term "homophobic homosexuals." Only men can be patriarchal, can be sexist. Only heterosexuals can be homophobic. The radical Black queer feminism of those two women detached homophobic from heterosexual, detached sexist from men and feminist from women, in the way I later detached racist from White people and antiracist from Black people. They had a problem with homophobia, not with heterosexuals. They had a problem with patriarchy, not with men. Crucially, their going after all homophobes, no matter their sexual identity, showed me that homophobic ideas and policies and power were their fundamental problem. Crucially, their going after all patriarchs, no matter their gender identity, showed me that patriarchal ideas and policies and powers were their fundamental problem. They talked of queer people defending homophobia as powerfully as they talked about heterosexuals building a world for queer love. They talked of women defending sexism as powerfully as men building a feminist world. Maybe they had me in mind. Because they opened that feminist world to me where queer love is wedded to heterosexual love, in harmony. But this world scared me like they scared me. Opened by them, I learned, though— and eventually I wanted to help them create that new world.

I am forever grateful that the Black graduate-student discourse was ruled by queer Black feminists instead of by patriarchal Black male homophobes. They were my first role models of Black feminism, of queer antiracism, of antiracist feminism. They met my homophobic patriarchy and forced me to meet him, too. Their force forced me to check his ass, as desperate as I was to stay out of the way of their attacks, a desperation that transformed into a curiosity about Black feminism and queer theory itself, a curiosity that transformed into a desire to be a gender antiracist, to be a queer antiracist, to not fail Black people—all Black people.

FAILURE

ACTIVIST: One who has a record of power or policy change.

T HE TEMPLE UNIVERSITY classroom started filling. Bodies hugging. Smiles and small talk and catching up. It all annoyed me as I sat, stood, and then sat again at the professor's desk, hoping to begin our Black Student Union (BSU) meeting on time. It was early September 2007. We were laughing and chatting in Philly, but that day, in Louisiana, six teenage lives hung in the balance. We had devised a campaign to free them. I was prepared to present it in order to secure organizers to execute it. I hardly suspected I was bound to fail.

To understand why racism lives is to understand the history of antiracist failure—why people have failed to create antiracist societies. To understand the racial history of failure is to understand failed solutions and strategies. To understand failed solutions and strategies is to understand their cradles: failed racial ideologies.

Incorrect conceptions of race as a social construct (as opposed to a power construct), of racial history as a singular march of racial progress (as opposed to a duel of antiracist and racist progress), of the race problem as rooted in ignorance and hate (as opposed to powerful self-interest)—all come together to produce solutions bound to fail. Terms and sayings like "I'm not racist" and "race neutral" and "post-racial" and "color-blind" and "only one race, the human race" and "only racists speak about race" and "Black people can't be racist" and "White people are evil" are bound to fail in identifying and eliminating racist power and policy. Stratagems flouting intersectionality are bound to fail the most degraded racial groups. Civilizing programs will fail since all racial groups are already on the same cultural level. Behavioral-enrichment programs, like mentoring and educational programs, can help individuals but are bound to fail racial groups, which are held back by bad policies, not bad behavior. Healing symptoms instead of changing policies is bound to fail in healing society. Challenging the conjoined twins separately is bound to fail to address economic-racial inequity. Gentrifying integration is bound to fail non-White cultures. All of these ideas are bound to fail because they have consistently failed in the past. But for some reason, their failure doesn't seem to matter: They remain the most popular conceptions and strategies and solutions to combat racism, because they stem from the most popular racial ideologies.

These repetitive failures exact a toll. Racial history does not repeat harmlessly. Instead, its devastation multiplies when generation after generation repeats the same failed strategies and solutions and ideologies, rather than burying past failures in the caskets of past generations.

—

EARLY WHITE ABOLITIONISTS met regularly at a national convention, thinking the antislavery solution rested in continuing "our parental care" over free Blacks, as they stated in 1805. White abolitionists lorded over Black behavior as if on good Black "conduct must, in some measure, depend the liberation of their brethren," as their convention stated in 1804.

The White judge birthed the Black judge. "The further decrease of prejudice, and the amelioration of the condition of thousands of our brethren who are yet in bondage, greatly depend on our conduct," Samuel Cornish and John Russwurm wrote on March 16, 1827, in one of the opening editorials of *Freedom's Journal*, the first African American newspaper.

I grew up on this same failed strategy more than one hundred fifty years later. Generations of Black bodies have been raised by the judges of "uplift suasion." The judges strap the entire Black race on the Black body's back, shove the burdened Black body into White spaces, order the burdened Black body to always act in an upstanding manner to persuade away White racism, and punish poor Black conduct with sentences of shame for reinforcing racism, for bringing the race down. I felt the burden my whole Black life to be perfect before both White people and the Black people judging whether I am representing the race well. The judges never let me just be, be myself, be my imperfect self.

—

IT FELT COOL outside, sometime in the autumn of 2011. Sadiqa and I had been dating for months. I looked at this Spelman sister and Georgia peach as a future wife: smitten by her affability as much as her elegance, by her perceptiveness as much as her easygoing sense of humor; smitten by her love of Black people as much as her love of saving human lives as a physician. She, too, had been raised in a middle-income Black home by similarly aged parents who cut their teeth in the movement, who brushed her teeth in the movement. She, too, had been taught that her climb up the success ladder uplifted the race. She, too, tried to represent the race well.

We dined near the window at Buddakan, an Asian fusion restaurant in Old City, Philadelphia. On the opposite wall, a massive gold statue of Buddha sat on a tiny stage at almost table level, against a red background that faded into a black center. Eyes closed. Hands clasped. At peace. Not bothering anyone. Certainly not Sadiqa. But the statue attracted a middle-aged, brown-haired, overweight White guy. Clearly drunk, he climbed onto the tiny stage and started fondling Buddha before his laughing audience of drunk friends at a nearby table. I had learned a long time ago to tune out the antics of drunk White people doing things that could get a Black person arrested. Harmless White fun is Black lawlessness.

His loud laughs summoned Sadiqa's look. "Oh, my God!" she said quietly. "What is this guy doing?"

She turned back to her plate, took a bite, and looked up as she swallowed. "At least he's not Black."

I was taken aback but immediately recognized myself—my own thoughts—in Sadiqa's face.

"How would you feel if he was Black?" I asked her, and myself.

"I'd be really embarrassed," she said, speaking for me and for so many of us trapped on the plantation of uplift suasion. "Because we don't need anyone making us look bad."

"In front of White people?" I asked her.

"Yes. It makes them look down on us. Makes them more racist."

We thought on a false continuum, from more racist to less racist to not racist. We believed good Black behavior made White people "less racist," even when our experiences told us it usually did not. But that night, we thought about it together and shared a few critiques of uplift suasion for the first time.

Today, the few critiques would be many. We would critique paternalistic White abolitionists conjuring up uplift suasion. We'd argue against the assumption that poor Black conduct is responsible for White racist ideas, meaning White racist ideas about poor Black conduct are valid. We'd critique the White judge exonerating White people from the responsibility to rid themselves of their own racist ideas; upwardly mobile Black people deflecting responsibility for changing racist policy by imagining they are uplifting the race by uplifting themselves; the near impossibility of perfectly executing uplift suasion, since Black people are humanly imperfect. We'd notice that when racist Whites see Black people conducting themselves admirably in public, they see those Blacks as extraordinary, meaning not like those ordinarily inferior Black people. We'd remember what history teaches us: that when racist policy knocks Black people down, the judge orders them to uplift themselves, only to be cut down again by racist terror and policy.

Sadiqa and I left the restaurant, but we continued to talk about the uplift-suasion ideology that had been so deeply ingrained in us—to critique it, critique ourselves, and run away from it, toward freedom. All these years later, although the judges can catch us at any moment, I admire Sadiqa's freedom to be Sadiqa. I feel free to move in my imperfections. I represent only myself. If the judges draw conclusions about millions of Black people based on how I act, then they, not I, not Black people, have a problem. They are responsible for their racist ideas; I am not. I am responsible for my racist ideas; they are not. To be antiracist is to let me be me, be myself, be my imperfect self.

—

ABOLITIONIST WILLIAM LLOYD Garrison did not let the Black body be her imperfect self. "Have you not acquired the esteem, confidence and patronage of the whites, in proportion to your increase in knowledge and moral improvement?" Garrison asked a Black crowd not long after founding *The Liberator* in 1831. Uplift suasion fit his ideology that the best way to "accomplish the great work of national redemption" from slavery was "through the agency of moral power" and truth and reason. Garrison's belief in "moral suasion" and what we can call "educational suasion" also fit his personal upbringing by a pious Baptist mother, his professional upbringing by an editor who believed newspapers are for "instruction," his abolitionist upbringing by moral crusader Benjamin Lundy.

Moral and educational and uplift suasion failed miserably in stopping the astounding growth of slavery in the age of King Cotton before the Civil War. But success, apparently, does not matter when a strategy stems from an ideology. Moral and educational suasion focus on persuading White people, on appealing to their moral conscience through horror and their logical mind through education. But what if racist ideas make people illogical?

What if persuading everyday White people is not persuading racist policymakers? What if racist policymakers know about the harmful outcomes of their policies? What if racist policymakers have neither morals nor conscience, let alone moral conscience, to paraphrase Malcolm X? What if no group in history has gained their freedom through appealing to the moral conscience of their oppressors, to paraphrase Assata Shakur? What if economic, political, or cultural self-interest drives racist policymakers, not hateful immorality, not ignorance?

"If I could save the Union without freeing any slave I would do it, and if I could save it by freeing all the slaves I would do that," President Abraham Lincoln wrote on August 20, 1862. "What I do about slavery, and the colored race, I do because I believe it helps to save the Union." On January 1, 1863, Lincoln signed the Emancipation Proclamation as a "necessary war measure." After winning the Civil War, racist Republicans (to distinguish from the less numerous antiracist Republicans) voted to establish the Freedmen's Bureau, reconstruct the South, and extend civil rights and voting privileges to create a loyal Southern Republican base and secure Black people in the South far away from northern Whites, who "want nothing to do with the negroes," as Illinois senator Lyman Trumbull, one of the laws' main sponsors, said.

The "White man's party," as Trumbull identified the Republican Party, grew "tired" of alienating their racist constituents by militarily defending the Negro from the racist terrorists who knocked Republicans out of Southern power by 1877. Republicans left Southern Blacks behind, turning their backs on the "outrages" of Jim Crow for nearly a century. "Expediency on selfish grounds, and not right with reference to the claims of our common humanity, has controlled our action," Garrison lamented in an address for the centennial of Independence Day, in 1876.

—

ON JUNE 26, 1934, W.E.B. Du Bois critically assessed the success of educational suasion, as Garrison had critically assessed moral suasion before him: "For many years it was the theory of most Negro leaders...that white America did not know of or realize the continuing plight of the Negro." Du Bois spoke for himself, believing "the ultimate evil was stupidity" early in his career. "Accordingly, for the last two decades, we have striven by book and periodical, by speech and appeal, by various dramatic methods of agitation, to put the essential facts before the American people. Today there can be no doubt that Americans know the facts; and yet they remain for the most part indifferent and unmoved."

Gunnar Myrdal ignored Du Bois's 1934 call for Black people to focus on accruing power instead of persuading White people. The racism problem lay in the "astonishing ignorance" of White Americans, Myrdal advised in *An American Dilemma* in 1944. "There is no doubt, in the writer's opinion, that a great majority of white people in America would be prepared to give the Negro a substantially better deal if they knew the facts."

Popular history tells us that a great majority of White Americans did give the Negro a better deal—the desegregation rulings, Civil Rights Act (1964), and Voting Rights Act (1965)—when they learned the facts. "Gunnar Myrdal had been astonishingly prophetic," according to one captivating history of the civil-rights movement. Not entirely. As early as 1946, top State Department official Dean Acheson warned the Truman administration that the "existence of discrimination against minority groups in this country has an adverse effect on our relations" with decolonizing Asian and African and Latin American nations. The Truman administration repeatedly briefed the U.S. Supreme Court on these adverse effects during desegregation cases in the late 1940s and early 1950s, as historian Mary L. Dudziak documents. Not to mention the racist abuse African diplomats faced in the United States. In 1963, Secretary of State Dean Rusk warned Congress during the consideration of the Civil Rights Act that "in waging this world struggle we are seriously handicapped by racial or religious discrimination." Seventy-eight percent of White Americans agreed in a Harris Poll.

Racist power started civil-rights legislation out of self-interest. Racist power stopped out of self-interest when enough African and Asian and Latin nations were inside the American sphere of influence, when a rebranded Jim Crow no longer adversely affected American foreign policy, when Black people started demanding and gaining what power rarely gives up: power. In 1967, Martin Luther King Jr. admitted, "We've had it wrong and mixed up in our country, and this has led Negro Americans in the past to seek their goals through love and moral suasion devoid of power." But our generation ignores King's words about the "problem of power, a confrontation between the forces of power demanding change and the forces of power dedicated to the preserving of the status quo." The same way King's generation ignored Du Bois's matured warning. The same way Du Bois's generation ignored Garrison's matured warnings. The problem of race has always been at its core the problem of power, not the problem of immorality or ignorance.

Moral and educational suasion breathes the assumption that racist minds must be changed before racist policy, ignoring history that says otherwise. Look at the soaring White support for desegregated schools and neighborhoods decades *after* the policies changed in the 1950s and 1960s. Look at the soaring White support for interracial marriage decades *after* the policy changed in 1967. Look at the soaring support for Obamacare *after* its passage in 2010. Racist policymakers drum up fear of antiracist policies through racist ideas, knowing if the policies are implemented, the fears they circulate will never come to pass. Once the fears do not come to pass, people will let down their guards as they enjoy the benefits. Once they clearly benefit, most Americans will support and become the defenders of the antiracist policies they once feared.

To fight for mental and moral changes *after* policy is changed means fighting alongside growing benefits and the dissipation of fears, making it possible for antiracist power to succeed. To fight for mental and moral change as a *prerequisite* for policy change is to fight against growing fears and apathy, making it almost impossible for antiracist power to succeed.

The original problem of racism has not been solved by suasion. Knowledge is only power if knowledge is put to the struggle for power. Changing minds is not a movement. Critiquing racism is not activism. Changing minds is not activism. An activist produces power and policy change, not mental change. If a person has no record of power or policy change, then that person is not an activist.

—

As I WAITED to begin the BSU meeting, I had already grown alienated about mental change. I wanted to be an activist. I wanted to flee academia. I wanted to free the Jena 6.

On September 1, 2006, the day after Black students had hung out under the "White tree" at Jena High School, White students hung nooses from its branches. The school's superintendent only suspended the White perpetrators for the "prank," which did nothing to curb the subsequent racial violence against Black students in the small town of Jena, Louisiana. But days after Black students beat up a White student on December 4, 2006, the Jena 6 were arrested. Jesse Ray Beard was charged as a juvenile. Robert Bailey Jr., Mychal Bell, Carwin Jones, Bryant Purvis, and Theo Shaw were charged with attempted murder. "When you are convicted, I will seek the maximum penalty allowed by law," promised district attorney Reed Walters, meaning up to one hundred years in prison.

As I sat at the teacher's desk, I felt Mychal Bell's sentencing hearing on September 20 approaching like the butcher's cleaver. An all-White jury had already found him guilty of a lesser charge, aggravated second-degree battery, lining up his life to be cut by as much as twenty-two years.

A somber energy settled inside the classroom, like the darkness outside. Our goal, BSU officers told each other, was to free the Jena 6. But were we willing to do anything? Were we willing to risk our freedom for their freedom? Not if our primary purpose was making ourselves feel better. We formulate and populate and donate to cultural and behavioral and educational enrichment programs to make ourselves feel better, feeling they are helping racial groups, when they are only helping (or hurting) individuals, when only policy change helps groups.

We arrive at demonstrations excited, as if our favorite musician is playing on the speakers' stage. We convince ourselves we are doing something to solve the racial problem when we are really doing something to satisfy our feelings. We go home fulfilled, like we dined at our favorite restaurant. And this fulfillment is fleeting, like a drug high. The problems of inequity and injustice persist. They persistently make us feel bad and guilty. We persistently do something to make ourselves feel better as we convince ourselves we are making society better, as we never make society better.

What if instead of a feelings advocacy we had an outcome advocacy that put equitable outcomes before our guilt and anguish? What if we focused our human and fiscal resources on changing power and policy to actually make society, not just our feelings, better?

—

I COULD WAIT no longer. I cut off the talking and smiling and began presenting the 106 Campaign to free the Jena 6. I began with phase one: Mobilize at least 106 students on 106 campuses in the mid-Atlantic to rally locally by the end of September and fundraise for the Jena 6 legal defense fund. I presented phase two: Marshal those 106 students from 106 campuses into car caravans that would converge on Washington, D.C., on October 5, 2007.

I painted the picture. "Wonderfully long lines of dozens of cars packed with students on highways and byways driving toward the nation's capital from all directions, from Pennsylvania, Delaware, Maryland, Virginia, West Virginia, and North Carolina." I stared but did not look into the eyes of my audience. I looked at the beautiful picture forming from my lips. "Thousands of cars with signs in the window —'Free the Jena Six'—honking to drivers passing by, who'd honk loudly back in solidarity (or revulsion).

"Can you see it?" I asked excitedly a few times.

They could see it. For some, the ugly picture.

"Isn't that illegal, the car caravans?" one woman asked, obviously scared.

"What? No! People take car caravans all the time," I replied.

I spoke on, painting the beautiful, ugly picture. "When the car caravans arrived in D.C., they would park their cars in the middle of Constitution Avenue and join the informal march to the Department of Justice. Thousands of cars would be sitting-in on Constitution Avenue and surrounding streets as we presented our six demands of freedom to the Bush administration. When they came with the tow trucks, we would be ready to flatten truck tires. When police units started protecting the tow trucks, we would come with reinforcements of cars. When they blocked off Constitution Avenue, we would strike another street with our cars. When and if they barricaded all the downtown streets, we would wait them out and ride back into downtown Washington whenever they lifted the barricades. We would refuse to stop the sit-in of cars until the Bush administration leaned on the Louisiana governor to lean on Jena officials to drop the charges against the Jena Six."

"This is illegal. They will throw us in prison," someone rebutted with a look of fear.

I should have stopped but I continued my failure, hardly caring that the more I spoke, the more fear I spread—the more fear I spread, the more I alienated people from the 106 Campaign.

"Damn right we could go to prison!" I shot back, feeling like myself. "But I don't care! We're already in prison. That's what America means: prison."

I used the Malcolm X line out of context. But who cared about context when the shock and awe sounded so radical to my self-identified radical ears? When I lashed out at well-meaning people who showed the normal impulse of fear, who used the incorrect racial terminology, who asked the incorrect question—oh, did I think I was so radical. When my scorched-earth words sent attendees fleeing at BSU rallies and meetings, when my scorched-earth writings sent readers fleeing, oh, did I think I was so radical. When in fact, if all my words were doing was sounding radical, then those words were not radical at all. What if we measure the radicalism of speech by how radically it transforms open-minded people, by how the speech liberates the antiracist power within? What if we measure the conservatism of speech by how intensely it keeps people the same, keeps people enslaved by their racist ideas and fears, conserving their inequitable society? At a time when I thought I was the most radical, I was the most conservative. I was a failure. I failed to address the fears of my BSU peers.

Fear is kind of like race—a mirage. "Fear is not real. It is a product of our imagination," as a Will Smith character tells his son in one of my favorite movies, *After Earth*. "Do not misunderstand me, danger is very real, but fear is a choice."

We do not have to be fearless like Harriet Tubman to be antiracist. We have to be courageous to be antiracist. Courage is the strength to do what is right in the face of fear, as the anonymous philosopher tells us. I gain insight into what's right from antiracist ideas. I gain strength from fear. While many people are fearful of what could happen if they resist, I am fearful of what could happen if I don't resist. I am fearful of cowardice. Cowardice is the inability to amass the strength to do what is right in the face of fear.

And racist power has been terrorizing cowardice into us for generations.

For segregationists like U.S. senator Ben "Pitchfork" Tillman, President Theodore Roosevelt crossed the color line when he dined with Booker T. Washington on October 16, 1901. "The action of President Roosevelt in entertaining that nigger will necessitate our killing a thousand niggers in the South before they will learn their place again." He was not joking.

On July 8, 1876, a young Tillman had joined the power-hungry White mob that murdered at least seven Black militiamen defending Black power in the Black town of Hamburg, South Carolina. All election year long, Tillman's Red Shirts had helped White supremacists violently snatch control of South Carolina. Tillman wore his involvement in the Hamburg Massacre as a badge of honor when he trooped on lynched heads into South Carolina's governorship in 1890 and the U.S. Senate in 1895. "The purpose of our visit to Hamburg was to strike terror," Tillman said at the Red Shirts reunion in 1909. As racist ideas intend to make us ignorant and hateful, racist terror intends to make us fear.

—

I WALKED OUT of that classroom building alone. I walked to the train station on the edge of campus, deciding on the long escalator down into the subway station that the BSU officers who voted down the 106 Campaign must be ignorant about racism, kind of like the White people supporting the Jena 6's incarceration. Deciding on the screeching train ride up to North Philadelphia that the "ultimate evil was ignorance" and "the ultimate good was education." Deciding as I lay flat on my couch and looked up at the ceiling mirror that a life of educational suasion would be more impactful than any other life I could choose.

I ran back down the lit path of educational suasion on the very night I failed to persuade my BSU peers. I failed at changing minds (let alone policy). But in all my enlightenment, I did not see myself as the failure. I saw my BSU peers as the failure. I did not look in the mirror at my "failure doctrine," the doctrine of failing to make change and deflecting fault.

When we fail to open the closed-minded consumers of racist ideas, we blame their closed-mindedness instead of our foolish decision to waste time reviving closed minds from the dead. When our vicious attacks on open-minded consumers of racist ideas fail to transform them, we blame their hate rather than our impatient and alienating hate of them. When people fail to consume our convoluted antiracist ideas, we blame their stupidity rather than our stupid lack of clarity. When we transform people and do not show them an avenue of support, we blame their lack of commitment rather than our lack of guidance. When the politician we supported does not change racist policy, we blame the intractability of racism rather than our support of the wrong politician. When we fail to gain support for a protest, we blame the fearful rather than our alienating presentation. When the protest fails, we blame racist power rather than our flawed protest. When our policy does not produce racial equity, we blame the people for not taking advantage of the new opportunity, not our flawed policy solution. The failure doctrine avoids the mirror of self-blame. The failure doctrine begets failure. The failure doctrine begets racism.

What if antiracists constantly self-critiqued our own ideas? What if we blamed our ideologies and methods, studied our ideologies and methods, refined our ideologies and methods again and again until they worked? When will we finally stop the insanity of doing the same thing repeatedly and expecting a different result? Self-critique allows change. Changing shows flexibility. Antiracist power must be flexible to match the flexibility of racist power, propelled only by the craving for power to shape policy in their inequitable interests. Racist power believes in by any means necessary. We, their challengers, typically do not, not even some of those inspired by Malcolm X. We care the most about the moral and ideological and financial purity of our ideologies and strategies and fundraising and leaders and organizations. We care less about bringing equitable results for people in dire straits, as we say we are purifying ourselves for the people in dire straits, as our purifying keeps the people in dire straits. As we critique the privilege and inaction of racist power, we show our privilege and inaction by critiquing every effective strategy, ultimately justifying our inaction on the comfortable seat of privilege. Anything but flexible, we are too often bound by ideologies that are bound by failed strategies of racial change.

What if we assessed the methods and leaders and organizations by their results of policy change and equity? What if strategies and policy solutions stemmed not from ideologies but from problems? What if antiracists were propelled only by the craving for power to shape policy in their equitable interests?

—

IN VOTING DOWN the 106 Campaign, the BSU officers crafted a different plan. They did something they did not fear. We loudly marched down North Broad Street and rallied on campus on September 20, 2007. That day, thousands of us thought we were protesting, when we were really demonstrating, from Philadelphia to Jena.

We use the terms "demonstration" and "protest" interchangeably, at our own peril, like we interchangeably use the terms "mobilizing" and "organizing." A protest is organizing people for a prolonged campaign that forces racist power to change a policy. A demonstration is mobilizing people momentarily to publicize a problem. Speakers and placards and posts at marches, rallies, petitions, and viral hashtags demonstrate the problem. Demonstrations are, not surprisingly, a favorite of suasionists. Demonstrations annoy power in the way children crying about something they will never get annoy parents. Unless power cannot economically or politically or professionally afford bad press—as power could not during the Cold War, as power cannot during election season, as power cannot close to bankruptcy—power typically ignores demonstrations.

The most effective demonstrations (like the most effective educational efforts) help people find the antiracist power within. The antiracist power within is the ability to view my own racism in the mirror of my past and present, view my own antiracism in the mirror of my future, view my own racial groups as equal to other racial groups, view the world of racial inequity as abnormal, view my own power to resist and overtake racist power and policy. The most effective demonstrations (like the most effective educational efforts) provide methods for people to give their antiracist power, to give their human and financial resources, channeling attendees and their funds into organizations and protests and power-seizing campaigns. The fundraising behind the scenes of the Jena 6 demonstrations secured better defense attorneys, who, by June 26, 2009, quietly got the charges reduced to simple battery, to guilty pleas, to no jail time for the accused.

As important as finding the antiracist power within and financial support, demonstrations can provide emotional support for ongoing protests. Nighttime rallies in the churches of Montgomery, Alabama, rocking with the courage-locking words of Martin Luther King Jr., sustained those courageous Black women who primarily boycotted the public buses and drained that revenue stream for the city throughout 1956.

The most effective protests create an environment whereby changing the racist policy becomes in power's self-interest, like desegregating businesses because the sit-ins are driving away customers, like increasing wages to restart production, like giving teachers raises to resume schooling, like passing a law to attract a well-organized force of donors or voters. But it is difficult to create that environment, since racist power makes laws that illegalize most protest threats. Organizing and protesting are much harder and more impactful than mobilizing and demonstrating. Seizing power is much harder than protesting power and demonstrating its excesses.

The demonstrations alone had little chance of freeing the Jena 6. A judge denied bail for one of the Jena 6 the day after the demonstrations. The news shocked and alienated some of my BSU peers from activism. After all, when we attend or organize demonstrations thinking they are protests, thinking they can change power and policy, and see no change happening, it is hard not to become cynical. It is hard not to think the Goliath of racism can never be defeated. It is hard to think of our strategies and solutions and ideologies and feelings as the true failures. It is hard to think we actually have all the tools for success.

CHAPTER 17

SUCCESS

FINANCE SCHOLAR BOYCE Watkins lectured on racism as a disease. I agonized over this conception. Not foundational enough, eternal enough, revolutionary enough on this eleventh evening of Black History Month in 2010. When the question-and-answer period arrived, I tossed up my arm from the back row, as Caridad smiled.

Caridad and I had been whispering for most of the lecture. For once, I felt confidence tingling in my head. Days before, Professor Asante had hooded me with my doctoral degree at Temple's commencement. The teen who hated school had finished graduate school in 2010, had committed himself to school for life.

Caridad was probably the one who ushered me to the lecture at SUNY Oneonta, our state college in the town of Oneonta, in upstate New York. Forgive me for calling Oneonta a town. Rural White people from surrounding areas labeled Oneonta "the city."

At Oneonta, Whiteness surrounded me like clouds from a plane's window, which didn't mean I found no White colleagues who were genial and caring. But it was Caridad, and all her Puerto Rican feminism and antiracism, who took me by the arm when I arrived as a dissertation fellow in 2008 and brought me closer when I stayed in 2009.

We were bound to become as close as our chairs. I filled the Black history post left vacant by Caridad's husband of eighteen years, Ralph. Metastatic cancer had taken Ralph's Black body in 2007. She probably could not look at me without seeing me standing in Ralph's shoes.

Her husband lost his fight to cancer but Caridad's life as an Afro-Latinx woman had brought its own fights—for peace, to be still. But she was a fighter, tireless and durable, as antiracists must be to succeed.

—

SUCCESS. THE DARK road we fear. Where antiracist power and policy predominate. Where equal opportunities and thus outcomes exist between the equal groups. Where people blame policy, not people, for societal problems. Where nearly everyone has more than they have today. Where racist power lives on the margins, like antiracist power does today. Where antiracist ideas are our common sense, like racist ideas are today.

Neither failure nor success is written. The story of our generation will be based on what we are willing to do. Are we willing to endure the grueling fight against racist power and policy? Are we willing to transform the antiracist power we gather within us to antiracist power in our society?

Caridad was willing, which strengthened my will. Caridad understood that even as her students struggled with racist and gender-racist and queer-racist and class-racist ideas, they also had within them the capacity to learn and change. She did not free the antiracist power within them with ideological attacks. Her classes were more like firm hugs tailored to each student's experience, compelling self-reflection. She took her Black and Latinx students—who were fighting their own anti-African cultural conditioning—to Ghana each year, where they found themselves eagerly immersed in their African ancestry by the trip's end. Meanwhile, I fought to survive at the intersections. The impulses of my bigoted past constantly threatened to take me back to the plantation of racist power. Caridad extended the arms of Kaila,

Yaba, and Weckea around me, ensuring I did not revert to my old thinking when I left Temple.

—

"INSTEAD OF DESCRIBING racism as a disease, don't you think racism is more like an organ?" I asked the lecturer. "Isn't racism essential for America to function? Isn't the system of racism essential for America to live?"

All my leading questions did not bait Boyce Watkins into a defense of his disease conception. Too bad. I wanted to engage him. I was not much of an intellectual. I closed myself off to new ideas that did not *feel* good. Meaning I shopped for conceptions of racism that fit my ideology and self-identity.

Asking antiracists to change their perspective on racism can be as destabilizing as asking racists to change their perspective on the races. Antiracists can be as doctrinaire in their view of racism as racists can be in their view of not-racism. How can antiracists ask racists to open their minds and change when we are closed-minded and unwilling to change? I ignored my own hypocrisy, as people customarily do when it means giving up what they hold dear. Giving up my conception of racism meant giving up my view of the world and myself. I would not without a fight. I would lash out at anyone who "attacked" me with new ideas, unless I feared and respected them like I feared and respected Kaila and Yaba.

—

I DERIVED MY perspective on racism from a book I first read in graduate school. When both Hillary Clinton and Bernie Sanders spoke of "institutional racism" on the presidential campaign trail in 2016, when the activists who demonstrated at their events spoke of "institutional racism," they were using, whether they realized it or not, a formulation coined in 1967 by Black Power activist

Kwame Toure and political scientist Charles Hamilton in *Black Power: The Politics of Liberation in America.*

"Racism is both overt and covert," Toure and Hamilton explained. "It takes two, closely related forms: individual whites acting against individual blacks, and acts by the total white community against the black community. We call these individual racism and institutional racism. The first consists of overt acts by individuals....The second type is less overt, far more subtle, less identifiable in terms of *specific* individuals committing the acts." They distinguished, for example, the individual racism of "white terrorists" who bomb a Black church and kill Black children from the institutional racism of "when in that same city—Birmingham, Alabama—five hundred black babies die each year because of the lack of proper food, shelter and medical facilities."

It is, as I thought upon first read, the gloomy system keeping us down and dead. The system's acts are covert, just as the racist ideas of the people are implicit. I could not wrap my head around the system or precisely define it, but I knew the system was there, like the polluted air in our atmosphere, poisoning Black people to the benefit of White people.

But what if the atmosphere of racism has been polluting most White people, too? And what if racism has been working in the opposite way for a handful of Black individuals, who find the fresh air of wealth and power in racist atmospheres? Framing institutional racism as acts by the "total White community against the total Black community" accounts for the ways White people benefit from racist policies when compared to their racial peers. (White poor benefit more than Black poor. White women benefit more than Black women. White gays benefit more than Black gays.) But this framing of White people versus Black people does *not* take into account that all White people do not benefit equally from racism. For instance, it doesn't take into account how rich Whites benefit more from racist policies than White poor and middle-income people. It does not take into account that Black people are not harmed equally by racism or that some Black individuals exploit racism to boost their own wealth and power.

But I did not care. I thought I had it all figured out. I thought of racism as an inanimate, invisible, immortal system, not as a living, recognizable, mortal disease of cancer cells that we could identify and treat and kill. I considered the system as essential to the United States as the Constitution. At times, I thought White people covertly operated the system, fixed it to benefit the total White community at the expense of the total Black community.

The construct of covert institutional racism opens American eyes to racism and, ironically, closes them, too. Separating the overt individual from the covert institutional veils the specific policy choices that cause racial inequities, policies made by specific people. Covering up the specific policies and policymakers prevents us from identifying and replacing the specific policies and policymakers. We become unconscious to racist policymakers and policies as we lash out angrily at the abstract bogeyman of "the system."

The perpetrators behind the five hundred Black babies dying each year in Birmingham "because of the lack of proper food, shelter and medical facilities" were no less overt than the "white terrorists" who killed four Black girls in a Birmingham church in 1963. In the way investigators can figure out exactly who those church bombers were, investigators can figure out exactly what policies caused five hundred Black babies to die each year and exactly who put those policies in place. In the way people have learned to see racist abuse coming out of the mouths of individual racists, people can learn to see racial inequities emerging from racist policies. All forms of racism are overt if our antiracist eyes are open to seeing racist policy in racial inequity.

But we do not see. Our eyes have been closed by racist ideas and the unacknowledged bond between the institutional antiracist and the post-racialist. They bond on the idea that institutional racism is often unseen and unseeable. Because it is covert, the institutional antiracist says. Because it hardly exists, the post-racialist says.

A similar bond exists between implicit bias and post-racialism. They bond on the idea that racist ideas are buried in the mind. Because they are implicit and unconscious, implicit bias says. Because they are dead, post-racialism says.

—

Toure and Hamilton could not have foreseen how their concepts of overt and covert racism would be used by people across the ideological board to turn racism into something hidden and unknowable. Toure and Hamilton were understandably focused on distinguishing the individual from the institutional. They were reacting to the same moderate and liberal and assimilationist forces that all these years later still reduce racism to the individual acts of White Klansmen and Jim Crow politicians and Tea Party Republicans and N-word users and White nationalist shooters and Trumpian politicos. " 'Respectable' individuals can absolve themselves from individual blame: they would never plant a bomb in a church; they would never stone a black family," Toure and Hamilton wrote. "But they continue to support political officials and institutions that would and do perpetuate institutionally racist policies."

The term "institutionally racist policies" is more concrete than "institutional racism." The term "racist policies" is more concrete than "institutionally racist policies," since "institutional" and "policies" are redundant: Policies are institutional. But I still occasionally use the terms "institutional racism" and "systemic racism" and "structural racism" and "overt" and "covert." They are like my first language of racism. But when we realize old words do not exactly and clearly convey what we are trying to describe, we should turn to new words. I struggle to concretely explain what "institutional racism" means to the Middle Eastern small businessman, the Black service worker, the White teacher, the Latinx nurse, the Asian factory worker, and the Native store clerk who do not take the courses on racism, do not read the books on racism, do not go to the lectures on racism, do not watch the specials on racism, do not listen to the podcasts on racism, do not attend the rallies against racism.

I try to keep everyday people in mind when I use "racist policies" instead of "institutional racism."

Policymakers and policies make societies and institutions, not the other way around. The United States is a racist nation because its policymakers and policies have been racist from the beginning. The conviction that racist policymakers can be overtaken, and racist policies can be changed, and the racist minds of their victims can be changed, is disputed only by those invested in preserving racist policymakers, policies, and habits of thinking.

Racism has always been terminal *and* curable. Racism has always been recognizable and mortal.

—

THE RAIN FELL on his gray hooded sweatshirt. It was February 26, 2012, a boring Sunday evening. I looked forward to my first book, on Black student activism in the late 1960s, being published in two weeks. The hooded teen looked forward to enjoying the watermelon juice and Skittles he'd purchased from a nearby 7-Eleven. The seventeen-year-old was easygoing, laid-back, like his strut. He adored LeBron James, hip-hop, and *South Park,* and dreamed of one day piloting airplanes.

Over six feet tall and lanky, Trayvon Martin ambled back in the rain to the Retreat at Twin Lakes. His father, Tracy Martin, had been dating a woman who lived in the gated community in Sanford, a suburb of Orlando, Florida. Tracy had brought along his son to talk to him, to refocus his mind on attending college like his older brother. Trayvon had just been suspended for carrying a bag with a trace of marijuana at his Miami high school. While suburban White teenage boys partied and drank and drove and smoked and snorted and assaulted to a chorus of "boys will be boys," urban Black boys faced zero tolerance in a policed state.

Martin dodged puddles on his slow stroll home. He called his girlfriend. He talked and walked through the front gate (or took a shortcut) into the cluster of sandy-colored two-story townhouses. As in many neighborhoods during the Great Recession, investors had been buying foreclosed properties and renting them out. With renters came unfamiliar faces, transient faces, and racists who connected the presence of Black teenagers with the "rash" of seven burglaries in 2011. They promptly organized a neighborhood-watch group.

The watch-group organizer was born a year after me, to a White Vietnam veteran and a Peruvian immigrant. Raised not far from where my family moved to in Manassas, Virginia, George Zimmerman moved to Florida as I did, after graduating high school. His assault conviction and domestic-violence accusations altered his plans to be a police officer. But nothing altered his conviction that the Black body—and not his own—was the criminal in his midst.

Zimmerman decided to run an errand. He hopped in his truck, his licensed slim 9-millimeter handgun tucked in a holster in his waistband. He drove. He noticed a hooded Black teenager walking through the complex. He dialed 911. The Black body's presence, a crime. The historic crime of racist ideas.

—

I DID NOT plan for my second book to be a history of racist ideas, as Zimmerman zeroed in on what could have been any Black male body, as he zeroed in on the teenager President Obama thought "could have been my son." After my first book, on the Black Campus Movement, I planned to research the student origins of Black studies in the 1960s. Then I realized that Black students were demanding Black studies because they considered all the existing disciplines to be racist. That the liberal scholars dominating those disciplines were refusing to identify their assimilationist ideas as racist. That they were identifying as not-racist, like the segregationists they were calling racist. That Black students were calling them both racist, redefining racist ideas. I wanted to write a long history using Black students' redefinition of racist ideas. But the daunting task scared me, like Zimmerman's glare scared Martin.

Martin called a friend and told his friend he was being followed. He picked up the pace. "Hey, we've had some break-ins in my neighborhood," Zimmerman told the 911 dispatcher. "And there's a real suspicious guy. This guy looks like he's up to no good, or he's on drugs or something....A dark hoodie, like a gray hoodie." He asked how long it would take for an officer to get there, because "these assholes, they always get away."

Martin ran. Zimmerman leapt out of his car in pursuit, gun at his waist, phone in hand. The dispatcher told him to stop. Zimmerman ended the call and caught up to Martin, a dozen or so minutes after 7:00 P.M. Only one person living knows exactly what happened next: Zimmerman, probably fighting to "apprehend" the "criminal." Martin probably fighting off the actual criminal for his life. Zimmerman squeezing the trigger and ending Martin's life. Claiming self-defense to save his own life. A jury agreeing, on July 13, 2013.

—

HEARTBROKEN, ALICIA GARZA typed "Black Lives Matter" into the mourning nights, into the Black caskets piling up before her as people shouted all those names from Trayvon Martin to Michael Brown to Sandra Bland to Korryn Gaines. The deaths and accusations and denials and demonstrations and deaths—it all gave me the strength each day to research for *Stamped from the Beginning*.

By the summer of 2012, I was finding and tagging every racist idea I could find from history. Racist ideas piled up before me like trash at a landfill. Tens of thousands of pages of Black people being trashed as natural or nurtured beasts, devils, animals, rapists, slaves, criminals, kids, predators, brutes, idiots, prostitutes, cheats, and dependents. More than five hundred years of toxic ideas on the Black body. Day after week, week after month, month after year, oftentimes twelve hours a day for three horrifically long years, I waded through this trash, consumed this trash, absorbed its toxicity, before I released a tiny portion of this trash onto the page.

All that trash, ironically, cleansed my mind if it did not cleanse my gut. While collecting this trash, I realized I had been unwittingly doing so my whole life. Some I had tossed away after facing myself in the mirror. Some trash remained. Like the dirty bags or traces of "them niggers" and "White people are devils" and "servile Asians" and "terrorist Middle Easterners" and "dangerous Black neighborhoods" and "weak Natives" and "angry Black women" and "invading Latinx" and "irresponsible Black mothers" and "deadbeat Black fathers." A mission to uncover and critique America's life of racist ideas turned into a mission to uncover and critique my life of racist ideas, which turned into a lifelong mission to be antiracist.

It happens for me in successive steps, these steps to be an antiracist.

I stop using the "I'm not a racist" or "I can't be racist" defense of denial.

I admit the definition of racist (someone who is supporting racist policies or expressing racist ideas).

I confess the racist policies I support and racist ideas I express.

I accept their source (my upbringing inside a nation making us racist).

I acknowledge the definition of antiracist (someone who is supporting antiracist policies or expressing antiracist ideas).

I struggle for antiracist power and policy in my spaces. (Seizing a policymaking position. Joining an antiracist organization or protest. Publicly donating my time or privately donating my funds to antiracist policymakers, organizations, and protests fixated on changing power and policy.)

I struggle to remain at the antiracist intersections where racism is mixed with other bigotries. (Eliminating racial distinctions in biology and behavior. Equalizing racial distinctions in ethnicities, bodies, cultures, colors, classes, spaces, genders, and sexualities.)

I struggle to think with antiracist ideas. (Seeing racist policy in racial inequity. Leveling group differences. Not being fooled into generalizing individual negativity. Not being fooled by misleading statistics or theories that blame people for racial inequity.)

Racist ideas fooled me nearly my whole life. I refused to allow them to continue making a fool out of me, a chump out of me, a slave out of me. I realized there is nothing wrong with any of the racial groups and everything wrong with individuals like me who think there is something wrong with any of the racial groups. It felt so good to cleanse my mind.

But I did not cleanse my body. I kept most of the toxic trash in my gut between 2012 and 2015. Did not talk about most of it. Tried to laugh it off. Did not address the pain of feeling the racist ideas butchering my Black body for centuries. But how could I worry about my body as I stared at police officers butchering the Black body almost every week on my cellphone? How could I worry about my body when racists blamed the dead, when the dead's loved ones cried and raged and numbed?

How could I worry about my suffering while Sadiqa suffered?

CHAPTER 18

SURVIVAL

S ADIQA AND I rarely sat on the rounded cream sofa in our new home in Providence. But our nerves brought us into the living room on this day in late August 2013.

We'd moved in weeks before as newlyweds. We eloped and changed our last names together months before, in a picturesque affair captured in *Essence*'s "Bridal Bliss" column. Sadiqa's gold dress and red accessories and cowrie-shell adornments and regal aura sitting on her throne of a peninsula beach as the waves bowed under the colorful sunset were all so sublime.

Still high from the pictures, we were crashing down now. We held hands, waiting for the phone call from the radiologist who performed the ultrasound and biopsy. A week prior, Sadiqa told me about the lump. She did not think much of it, probably knowing that 93 percent of women diagnosed with breast cancer are over forty years old. She was thirty-four. But she obliged my requests to see a doctor that day. The phone rang. We jumped as if we were watching a horror flick. On speakerphone, the doctor said Sadiqa had invasive breast cancer.

Minutes later, we were upstairs. Sadiqa could not do it. I had to call and tell a mother who had lost a daughter that her living daughter had cancer. I stood in our guest room as her mother let out a wail, as Sadiqa wailed in our bedroom, as I wailed in my mind.

The wailing soon stopped, if the worry encircling and suffocating my wife did not. Sadiqa surveyed the fight ahead. Surgery to remove the lump. Chemotherapy to prevent a recurrence. Close monitoring to notice and treat a recurrence.

Sadiqa had time before surgery. We decided to freeze embryos in case the chemotherapy harmed her ovaries. The process dangerously overstimulated her ovaries, filling her abdomen with fluid, causing a blood clot. We slept in the hospital for a week as she recovered. All before her cancer fight.

The blood clot made doing surgery first too dangerous. Chemotherapy came first, which meant three months of watching and feeling her anguish. She was a foodie who couldn't really taste her food. She had to push through chronic fatigue to exercise. She'd just completed twelve years of medical training, but now instead of seeing patients, she'd become one herself. It was like training hard for a marathon and getting sick steps into the race. But she kept running: through chemotherapy, through three surgeries, through another year of less toxic chemotherapy. And she won.

—

I HAD TROUBLE separating Sadiqa's cancer from the racism I studied. The two consumed my life over the final months of 2013 and during the better part of 2014 and 2015. Months after Sadiqa survived stage-2 breast cancer, Ma was diagnosed with stage-1 breast cancer. She endured radiation and a lumpectomy in 2015. Those years were all about caretaking Sadiqa, helping Dad caretake Ma, and—when they were sleeping or enjoying company or desiring alone time—retreating from the pain of their cancer into the stack of racist ideas I'd collected.

Over time, the source of racist ideas became obvious, but I had trouble acknowledging it. The source did not fit my conception of racism, my racial ideology, my racial identity. I became a college professor to educate away racist ideas, seeing ignorance as the source of racist ideas, seeing racist ideas as the source of racist policies, seeing mental change as the principal solution, seeing myself, an educator, as the primary solver.

Watching Sadiqa's courage to break down her body to rebuild her body inspired me to accept the source of racist ideas I found while researching their entire history —even though it upended my previous way of thinking. My research kept pointing me to the same answer: The source of racist ideas was not ignorance and hate, but self-interest.

The history of racist ideas is the history of powerful policymakers erecting racist policies out of self-interest, then producing racist ideas to defend and rationalize the inequitable effects of their policies, while everyday people consume those racist ideas, which in turn sparks ignorance and hate. Treating ignorance and hate and expecting racism to shrink suddenly seemed like treating a cancer patient's symptoms and expecting the tumors to shrink. The body politic might feel better momentarily from the treatment—from trying to eradicate hate and ignorance—but as long as the underlying cause remains, the tumors grow, the symptoms return, and inequities spread like cancer cells, threatening the life of the body politic. Educational and moral suasion is not only a failed strategy. It is a suicidal strategy.

—

THIS MESSAGE OF focusing on policy change over mental change was written in my next book, *Stamped from the Beginning*. After the book came out in 2016, I took this message on the road from our new home at the University of Florida. I talked about racist policies leading to racist ideas, not the other way around, as we have commonly thought. I talked about eliminating racist policies if we ever hope to eliminate racist ideas. I talked and talked, unaware of my new hypocrisy, which readers and attendees picked up on. "What are *you* doing to change policy?" they kept asking me in public and private.

I started questioning myself. What am I doing to change policy? How can I genuinely urge people to focus on changing policy if I am not focused on changing policy? Once again, I had to confront and abandon a cherished idea.

I did not need to forsake antiracist research and education. I needed to forsake my orientation to antiracist research and education. I had to forsake the suasionist bred into me, of researching and educating for the sake of changing minds. I had to start researching and educating to change policy. The former strategy produces a public scholar. The latter produces public scholarship.

—

IN THE SUMMER of 2017, I moved to American University in the nation's capital to found and direct the Antiracist Research and Policy Center. My research in the history of racism and antiracism revealed that scholars, policy experts, journalists, and advocates had been crucial in successfully replacing racist policy with antiracist policy.

I envisioned building residential fellowship programs and bringing to Washington dream teams of scholars, policy experts, journalists, and advocates, who would be assisted by classrooms of students from the nation's most politically active student body. The teams would focus on the most critical and seemingly intractable racial inequities. They would investigate the racist policies causing racial inequity, innovate antiracist policy correctives, broadcast the research and policy correctives, and engage in campaigns of change that work with antiracist power in locales to institute and test those policy correctives before rolling them out nationally and internationally.

These teams would model some of the steps we can all take to eliminate racial inequity in our spaces.

> *Admit racial inequity is a problem of bad policy, not bad people.*
>
> *Identify racial inequity in all its intersections and manifestations.*
>
> *Investigate and uncover the racist policies causing racial inequity.*
>
> *Invent or find antiracist policy that can eliminate racial inequity.*
>
> *Figure out who or what group has the power to institute antiracist policy.*
>
> *Disseminate and educate about the uncovered racist policy and antiracist policy correctives.*
>
> *Work with sympathetic antiracist policymakers to institute the antiracist policy.*
>
> *Deploy antiracist power to compel or drive from power the unsympathetic racist policymakers in order to institute the antiracist policy.*
>
> *Monitor closely to ensure the antiracist policy reduces and eliminates racial inequity.*
>
> *When policies fail, do not blame the people. Start over and seek out new and more effective antiracist treatments until they work.*
>
> *Monitor closely to prevent new racist policies from being instituted.*

On the September night I unveiled the vision of the Antiracism Center before my peers at American University, racist terror unveiled its vision, too. After my presentation, during my late-night class, an unidentified, middle-aged, hefty White male, dressed in construction gear, posted copies of Confederate flags with cotton balls inside several buildings. He posted them on the bulletin boards outside my classroom. The timing did not seem coincidental. I ignored my fears and pressed on during the final months of 2017. This wasn't the only thing I put out of my mind. I also ignored my weight loss and pressed on. It became annoying going in and out of bathrooms only to produce nothing, only to still feel like I needed to go minutes later. But I felt I had more important matters to worry about. After all, White nationalists were running and terrorizing the United States and their power was spreading across the Western world.

I did not have a rejuvenating break during Thanksgiving. I was bedridden. The throwing up started and stopped after the weekend. The bloody diarrhea did not. It all became worse. By Christmas, things had become acute. I obliged when Sadiqa urged me to get myself checked out.

Neither the nurse practitioner nor Sadiqa thought it was anything serious. I was thirty-five, about half the median age for the worst possibility, colon cancer. I did not exhibit any of the risk factors for colon cancer, since I exercised, rarely drank, never smoked, and had been a vegan since Sadiqa and I made the change to help prevent a recurrence of her cancer. We scheduled a precautionary colonoscopy for January 10, 2018.

—

I WAS GROGGY from the anesthesia early that morning. Cleaning out my colon had been an all-night affair. Sadiqa helped me put on my clothes in the small and dreary consultation room. No windows or striking colors or decorations, only pictures of the GI tract hanging on the walls. The Black woman doctor who'd performed the colonoscopy entered the room with a serious look on her face.

"I saw something abnormal," she said, sitting down. "I saw a mass in the sigmoid colon. It is large and friable, and it is bleeding." I looked at her in confusion, not knowing what she meant. Sadiqa looked at her in shock, knowing exactly what she meant.

She said she could not get her scope past the mass. It was obstructing the colon. "It is most likely cancerous," she said.

She paused as my confusion converted into shock. I checked out of myself. Sadiqa had to speak for me, really listen for me. The doctor told me to get blood work that day and get my body scanned the next day to confirm the cancer. I did not know what to think or feel. And so I did not feel or think anything other than shock.

At one point, several minutes later, perhaps as someone drained me of blood, I thought about Professor Mazama. About when I told her Sadiqa's diagnosis and asked, "Why her?"

"Why not her?" Professor Mazama responded.

Why not me?

I thought of Sadiqa and Ma and Dad's cancer fights. *Why not me?* They survived. *Why shouldn't I be the one to die?*

—

WE LEFT THE medical office in downtown Washington and headed for Busboys and Poets to meet Ma for breakfast. We sat down at the table. Ma had been waiting for a half hour. She asked why it took so long. I was still mute, looking down, up, away from anyone's eyes. Sadiqa told Ma about the mass. That it was probably cancer. "Okay, if it is, we will deal with it," Ma said. I looked up into her eyes, holding back tears. "We will deal with it," she said again. I knew she was serious. "Yes, we will," Sadiqa said, snatching my eyes. *Yes, we will,* I said to myself, absorbing their courage.

That night, I received more courage, when Sadiqa and I assumed we'd caught the cancer early. Probably stage 1 or 2. Perhaps 3. Not stage 4. About 88 percent of people diagnosed with stage-4 colon cancer die within five years.

The next day, they confirmed it. I had metastatic colon cancer. Stage 4. *Maybe we won't be able to deal with it.*

—

OUR WORLD IS suffering from metastatic cancer. Stage 4. Racism has spread to nearly every part of the body politic, intersecting with bigotry of all kinds, justifying all kinds of inequities by victim blaming; heightening exploitation and misplaced hate; spurring mass shootings, arms races, and demagogues who polarize nations; shutting down essential organs of democracy; and threatening the life of human society with nuclear war and climate change. In the United States, the metastatic cancer has been spreading, contracting, and threatening to kill the American body as it nearly did before its birth, as it nearly did during its Civil War. But how many people stare inside the body of their nations' racial inequities, their neighborhoods' racial inequities, their occupations' racial inequities, their institutions' racial inequities, and flatly deny that their policies are racist? They flatly deny that racial inequity is the signpost of racist policy. They flatly deny the racist policy as they use racist ideas to justify the racial inequity. They flatly deny the cancer of racism as the cancer cells spread and literally threaten their own lives and the lives of the people and spaces and places they hold dear. The popular conception of denial—like the popular strategy of suasion—is suicidal.

—

I HAD BEEN thinking all week about denial, before the diagnosis, after the diagnosis. I still could not separate racism and cancer. I sat in the waiting rooms, between medical meetings, tests, and procedures, writing an essay arguing that the heartbeat of racism is denial, the heartbeat of antiracism is confession. It appeared in *The New York Times* on Sunday, January 14, 2018, three days after my diagnosis. But my writing on the denial of racism did not stop me from denying the severity of my cancer. I could not confess I was likely to die.

I had been privately making sense of racism through cancer since Sadiqa's diagnosis. Except now I started making sense out of my cancer through my new conception of racism. Denying my ability to succeed in my cancer fight did not differ from those denying our ability to succeed in the antiracism fight. Denial is much easier than admission, than confession.

I have cancer. The most serious stage. Cancer is likely to kill me. I can survive cancer against all odds.

My society has racism. The most serious stage. Racism is likely to kill my society. My society can survive racism against all odds.

I prepared myself to fight. I looked past what could harm me in the fight to see all that could bring me joy if I survived. Dancing through life with my surviving and thriving partner. Watching my nearly two-year-old Black girl grow into a phenomenal woman. Growing myself into a better self through the love of my constructive family and friends and mentors I know and do not know. Engaging the open-minded readers of *Stamped from the Beginning*. Building the Antiracism Center into an intellectual factory of antiracist policy. Witnessing my beloved New York Knicks finally win an NBA championship. Writing for *The Atlantic,* in the same pages as W.E.B. Du Bois. Finishing this book and sharing it with the world.

I looked at the antiracist progress coming in my lifetime, the antiracist society coming in my granddaughter's lifetime, our great-grandchildren refusing to return to the racist time when all the victims of all forms of bigotries that feed and are fed by racism had far less resources, far less of an opportunity to be one with their humanity, to be one with human difference, to be one with our shared humanity.

—

MY TREATMENT PLAN took shape like battle plans. Six months of chemotherapy. If my tumors shrank, the chance for surgery. The chance of removing the rest of the tumors. The chance at life if there was not a recurrence. A long shot. But a chance.

On Mondays, every three weeks, beginning in late January 2018, I received chemo injections and started taking two weeks of chemo pills. By Tuesdays, I already felt like I had been jumped by Smurf and his boys. Could barely climb out of bed. Could barely write this book. Could barely eat and drink. But I pushed myself to get out of bed, to write, to stay hydrated, because when I did not exercise my body and mind, when I did not consume enough protein and thoughts and fluids, I could feel the toxicity levels rising in my body, exacerbating all the symptoms.

To keep up with my normal life, I had to go outside into the bitter cold of winter, not merely to the gym but to meetings, to speaking engagements, to life. The chemo made me hypersensitive to cold. Thirty degrees outside felt like negative ten degrees inside me. Whenever I breathed in cold air, it hurt my lungs. Whenever I drank ice-cold fluids, it hurt my throat. Whenever I touched anything cold, it hurt my fingers.

Instead of wallowing in the chronic discomfort or asking the doctor to ease the chemo, I found ways to make myself more comfortable. Pain is usually essential to healing. When it comes to healing America of racism, we want to heal America without pain, but without pain, there is no progress.

—

MY TUMORS SHRANK enough for me to go on the surgical table by the end of the summer of 2018. Surgeons removed what was left and sewed me back together. Pathologists dissected what they took out and did not find any cancer cells. The six months of chemotherapy had obliterated, apparently, all the cancer. My doctors were as shocked as I had been when I was diagnosed. I had a good chance to land in the 12 percent of people who survived stage-4 colon cancer.

—

WE CAN SURVIVE metastatic racism. Forgive me. I cannot separate the two, and no longer try. What if humanity connected the two? Not just the number of people of all races who would not die each year from cancer if we launched a war against cancer instead of against bodies of color who kill us in far lesser numbers. Not just the better prevention and treatment options doctors would have if we diverted to cancer care and research a portion of the trillions of tax dollars we spend on cutting taxes for the rich, imprisoning people, bombing people, and putting troops in harm's way.

What if we treated racism in the way we treat cancer? What has historically been effective at combatting racism is analogous to what has been effective at combatting cancer. I am talking about the treatment methods that gave me a chance at life, that give millions of cancer fighters and survivors like me, like you, like our loved ones, a chance at life. The treatment methods that gave millions of our relatives and friends and idols who did not survive cancer a chance at a few more days, months, years of life. What if humans connected the treatment plans?

Saturate the body politic with the chemotherapy or immunotherapy of antiracist policies that shrink the tumors of racial inequities, that kill undetectable cancer cells. Remove any remaining racist policies, the way surgeons remove the tumors. Ensure there are clear margins, meaning no cancer cells of inequity left in the body politic, only the healthy cells of equity. Encourage the consumption of healthy foods for thought and the regular exercising of antiracist ideas, to reduce the likelihood of a recurrence. Monitor the body politic closely, especially where the tumors of racial inequity previously existed. Detect and treat a recurrence early, before it can grow and threaten the body politic.

But before we can treat, we must believe. Believe all is not lost for you and me and our society. Believe in the possibility that we can strive to be antiracist from this day forward. Believe in the possibility that we can transform our societies to be antiracist from this day forward. Racist power is not godly. Racist policies are not indestructible. Racial inequities are not inevitable. Racist ideas are not natural to the human mind.

Race and racism are power constructs of the modern world. For roughly two hundred thousand years, before race and racism were constructed in the fifteenth century, humans saw color but did not group the colors into continental races, did not commonly attach negative and positive characteristics to those colors and rank the races to justify racial inequity, to reinforce racist power and policy. Racism is not even six hundred years old. It's a cancer that we've caught early.

But racism is one of the fastest-spreading and most fatal cancers humanity has ever known. It is hard to find a place where its cancer cells are not dividing and multiplying. There is nothing I see in our world today, in our history, giving me hope that one day antiracists will win the fight, that one day the flag of antiracism will fly over a world of equity. What gives me hope is a simple truism. Once we lose hope, we are guaranteed to lose. But if we ignore the odds and fight to create an antiracist world, then we give humanity a chance to one day survive, a chance to live in communion, a chance to be forever free.